Your Sacred Adoption

Your Sacred Adoption

✦

A Guided Journal of Life, Love and Memories

Kevin Quirk

iUniverse, Inc.
New York Lincoln Shanghai

Your Sacred Adoption
A Guided Journal of Life, Love and Memories

Copyright © 2008 by Kevin Quirk

iUniverse books may be ordered through booksellers or by contacting:

iUniverse
2021 Pine Lake Road, Suite 100
Lincoln, NE 68512
www.iuniverse.com
1-800-Authors (1-800-288-4677)

Because of the dynamic nature of the Internet, any Web addresses or links contained in this book may have changed since publication and may no longer be valid.

The views expressed in this work are solely those of the author and do not necessarily reflect the views of the publisher, and the publisher hereby disclaims any responsibility for them.

ISBN: 978-0-595-48530-7 (pbk)
ISBN: 978-0-595-60625-2 (ebk)

Printed in the United States of America

Contents

Introduction

Bringing any child into the world is, as any parent knows, an experience deserving of the deepest respect and reverence—something sacred. But as an adoptive parent, or someone considering adoption, you know well that bringing a child into your life through adoption is a unique sacred endeavor. When you adopt a child, you step into a world of joys and challenges, wrapped in layers of trust, adventure, risk, sacrifice, perseverance, mystery, and awe.

Adoption opens our hearts, stirs our deepest feelings, and leaves us shaking our heads at wonder at how it all comes together. If you have already made, or may be making, this wondrous leap of faith, it's natural to want to preserve all your most meaningful memories, experiences, and feelings, so that you may have a treasured keepsake for you and your child. This journal will provide you the opportunity to capture all those special moments, to give voice to them, and to make sure you will always have them to remember and appreciate. From that initial spark that first told you that adoption may become part of your life, to your favorite bedtime rituals at home with your child months or years down the road, you will find in the pages ahead a simple and easy way to record, to honor, and to reflect upon this life-transforming experience.

As an adoptive parent of a 6-year-old boy from Kazakhstan, I understand just how fast this all goes by. One minute you're trying to navigate your way through mounds of paper work just to get the whole adoption process started, and the next minute you're celebrating Adoption Day, or "Gotcha" Day, for the fifth time. Or so it seems. It's easy to get so caught up in what you have to do to make adoption a reality and begin this new life together that you lose touch with *why* you're doing this or what it really means. Later, when you try to recapture everything that happened to you and your child, and how you felt about it, you sometimes discover that many of your memories have become vague or even lost. Keeping this detailed journal as you go along, or soon after the experience, will ensure that you will preserve what really matters to you.

By filling in your responses to each of the short phrases, you will be offering a wonderful gift for your child. This book will help them understand a broad range of experiences of how they came to be with you. It will not only provide them with a wealth of important information about their adoption, it will also tell them the *story* behind it all, and how that story has shaped you and them. By faithfully and honestly recording your responses now, you will be helping to lay the foundation for your child to know, to understand, and to share that story later. Your responses may become part of an adoption lifebook for your child.

Also, by focusing on the sacred aspects of your adoption, you're offering your child a beautiful reflection of who they really are and how they are loved. You're helping them see the magic, the mystery, and the awe behind their early life. And by sharing your own feelings about everything that happens along the way, you open a door to further communication with your child about the sacred bonds that unite you. As a bonus, you will be enriching your own appreciation of all the experiences that touched you. Writing in this book may prompt new and important discoveries that guide you in your own sacred journey.

I want to say a few words about terms like "spirit" or "God" or "the sacred" as they are used in this journal. In earning a Masters degree in Spiritual Psychology many years ago, I gained a deeper appreciation of the basic truths of all religions, faiths, and spiritual traditions. My hope is that you may feel at home following the course of this journal no matter what religion, belief system, or spiritual orientation you may be guided by. You may be a devout Christian and see everything that unfolds in your life through that lens. You may be connected to the Jewish tradition. Your spiritual roots may be rooted in other cultures, or you may have integrated the teachings from many spiritual beliefs and practices. Even if you don't follow any specific religion, I hope that you may feel welcome here. Somehow you resonated with the term "sacred" in the title of this book, so I trust that you will find it useful in preserving your memories. If we look at the sacred as being a part of something bigger than ourselves, we are likely to conclude it's a universal experience.

Whatever your religion or spiritual beliefs, I invite you to use this journal to make it meaningful and reflective of how *you* look at life and what matters most to you. If that means changing a word or phrase that I have chosen in any subject or phrase to make it more consistent with your faith or principles, by all means feel free to do so. And if that leads you to pass on one or more of the suggested phrases because it doesn't seem to speak to you, that's fine too. This is *your* journal for *your* family. Do whatever it takes to make it truly yours!

I also hope that you find this journal a useful tool whatever route of adoption you followed. While I adopted internationally, I have met many, many others who have adopted domestically and through many different channels. Again, you may need to substitute some words or terms to make them best fit your adoption process. I also sought to write in a voice that speaks to married adoptive parents, single adoptive mothers, or anyone else whose life has been touched by adoption. And the fill-in prompts you will follow should be relevant for children adopted at any age: infants, toddlers, older children, etc.

The journal is divided into five sections, or phases of your adoption experience:

• Sacred Inspiration—Saying Yes!

• Sacred Anticipation—Getting Ready

• Sacred Celebration—Making It Happen

• Sacred Beginnings—Starting a New Life

• Sacred Commitment—Keeping Spirit Alive

If you haven't begun your adoption process, you will be able to chart your experiences in each phase as they unfold. But don't worry if you notice that you're already in the second, third, or even the final phase. When you read and reflect upon the phrases in each section, your memories and feelings will come back.

For some of you, journaling in response to open-ended phrases may be a familiar practice. For others, it may feel new and different. In the classes I teach on writing your life story, I find that anyone, regardless of experience, can find this kind of writing exercise easy, useful, enjoyable, meaningful—and often full of surprises! You will find that the prompts usually work best if you write spontaneously, with the first thought that comes to mind, rather than trying to think it all out and craft the "perfect" response. Your heart knows what you most need to say, and preserve. Trust it. Over time, you might even notice yourself wanting to add your own prompts to get down something else important to you that I left out. Go right ahead!

In recording your responses, some of you may find it natural and easy to write directly in this book. That's fine. Some of you may decide that you'd be more comfortable writing your answers in your own personal journal, which you can decorate your way from cover to end, and use all the space you need for longer answers. Others may prefer a three-ring binder that you can more easily open up and lay flat. And I'm sure there are many of you who simply couldn't imagine writing anything if it's not on your laptop! You should find that the phrases are short and simple enough to quickly copy into your computer or personal journal and then move right on to your responses.

I devised this journal a few years after writing and publishing my own book about our adoption experience, *Hello, Aibek! A Journey of International Adoption*. Even after writing that memoir, I wished I had had a journal like this one to help chronicle our experience from the perspective of the sacred and spiritual. Perhaps this is something you've also been looking for too. If finding this book in any way answers your hopes or prayers, I would be deeply touched.

Reflecting on and writing about your adoption as a sacred experience is, of course, a personal endeavor. You may decide not to share what you're doing with anyone until you feel complete with it. After you've finished, you may of course want to begin to share it with loved ones and others. And if you feel called to share it with an even broader community of those whose lives have been or will be enriched by adoption, I'd certainly welcome hearing from you. Perhaps enough of us may even choose to be a part of a shared book: Our Sacred Adoption Stories.

Many blessings to you all!

Kevin Quirk

Memoirs for Life (www.memoirsforlife.com)

kevin@memoirsforlife.com

Sacred Inspiration—Saying Yes!

Think back to that special moment when you first had an idea that adoption might become a part of your life. Recall the time, the place, the circumstances, and the people around you.

I first wanted to adopt a child because

Your Nana loved children with all of who she was even if they weren't her own. She always welcomed others into our family with no boundaries between "us" and "them." This acceptance of others taught me how to love and opened my understanding for the great need to love others -Mommy

Something telling me that this was "meant to be" was

When I met your Daddy and found out that not only would he be willing to adopt but that he himself was adopted. -Mommy

Once I began taking steps toward adoption, I was the most excited about

meeting my kids; I wonder about how old
you are, what you look like, where you live,
and what are life will be like together. I am
also very excited about showing you off,
loving you, teaching you, and holding you
close. —Mommy

I was the most concerned or uncertain about

I am afraid that we wont be approved to
adopt. This is scary because I already
love you so much and want to bring you
home to our family. Daddy had a tough time
with work last year and I get scared that
this would make others think we cant provide
for you. Right now the application process is
very intimidating.

Some new hopes and dreams stirred in me were

New hopes that you have inspired include learning how to love more unconditionally, learning about others, loving your birth family, teaching you about our faith and family. I'm really excited about traveling with you and seeing new things together. — Mommy

Former hopes and dreams I had to let go of were

I needed to let go of my expectations about what you would be when you grow up, that you might not want to go to university like I did and that you won't look like the picture in my head. I had to let go of the timing about when you would become part of our family. — Mommy

Now consider the most important people with whom you shared your plan to adopt: your spouse or partner, your family, your friends, your community.

The people I most often turned to for support or guidance were

Daddy, Nana, Aunty Kori, Aunty Kathryn, Aunty Jen m, and Aunty Lacey. They helped me have faith and keep going. Aunty Carrea helped me believe in myself and trust my love for you. - Mommy

What they did or said that really touched me was

Aunty Kathryn got us this book.
Aunty Kori told me I could do it and was called for this.
Nana was so excited to have you come home.
Aunty Jen m told me she would help with whatever you needed.
Daddy wants you as much as I do.

One new friendship that emerged from my decision to adopt was

_____
_____
_____
_____
_____
_____
_____
_____
_____
_____
_____
_____

Next, recall your process of choosing the method of adoption you would follow (domestic, international, etc.) and the place where it would happen.

I chose the adoption process that was best for me by

_____
_____
_____
_____
_____
_____
_____
_____
_____
_____
_____
_____
_____
_____

The person who most influenced me in my decision, and how they helped was

_____

_____

_____

_____

_____

_____

_____

_____

_____

_____

_____

_____

_____

_____

One message from God or spirit was

_____

_____

_____

_____

_____

_____

_____

_____

_____

_____

_____

_____

_____

_____

Close your eyes for a moment. Consider your whole experience of putting your inspiration to adopt into motion.

Considering everything that's happened, what first makes me want to laugh or smile about my adoption process now is

_____
_____
_____
_____
_____
_____
_____
_____
_____
_____
_____
_____

What makes me want to cry or sigh about it all is

_____
_____
_____
_____
_____
_____
_____
_____
_____
_____
_____
_____

Take a moment to reflect on the following qualities and the role they played during your Sacred Inspiration:

Trust:

I had to most show trust when

_____

_____

_____

Grief:

I felt the most grief over

_____

_____

_____

Mystery:

I felt the greatest sense of mystery when

_____

_____

_____

Expectancy:

The expectancy I felt as I looked ahead to adoption was like

_____

_____

_____

Use this page to add your own photos, drawings, inspirational messages, or other keepsakes that relate to Saying Yes to your adoption:

Sacred Anticipation—Getting Ready

Recall the many steps you took in preparing for your adoption: educating your family about what to expect, the paperwork, the legal procedures, your agency/attorney selection, your home study visit, reading resource books, taking adoption classes & workshops, your financial adjustments, preparing your child's room, joining adoption-oriented Listservs, etc.

What I most enjoyed about the time of getting ready to adopt was

_____

_____

_____

_____

_____

_____

_____

The most difficult or frustrating part was

_____

_____

_____

_____

_____

_____

One person or message that kept me going was

_____
_____
_____
_____
_____
_____
_____
_____
_____
_____
_____
_____
_____
_____

The best advice I received in preparing for adoption was

_____
_____
_____
_____
_____
_____
_____
_____
_____
_____
_____
_____
_____
_____
_____
_____

One pivotal or magical moment that told me that I was doing the right thing was

_____
_____
_____
_____
_____
_____
_____
_____
_____
_____
_____

Remember back to when you first saw or heard anything about your child, including your child's birth mother, living environment, or the group from which your child would be selected.

What surprised me the most related to what I learned about you or where you came from was

_____
_____
_____
_____
_____
_____
_____
_____
_____
_____
_____

One coincidence or sign of "rightness" related to names, birth dates, physical appearance or other factors that was telling me that you were meant to be *my* child was

_____
_____
_____
_____
_____
_____
_____
_____
_____
_____
_____
_____
_____

If I received a referral, what most led me to say yes to you was

_____
_____
_____
_____
_____
_____
_____
_____
_____
_____
_____
_____
_____

I told others the news by

_____
_____
_____
_____
_____
_____
_____
_____
_____
_____
_____
_____

Having feelings of love for a child I had never met was like

_____
_____
_____
_____
_____
_____
_____
_____
_____
_____
_____
_____
_____
_____

Now recall those last days of preparing for your intercountry adoption trip, hospital liaison, or other arrangement for your adoption placement.

What I most remember about those final days or hours was

_____

_____

_____

_____

_____

_____

_____

_____

_____

_____

_____

_____

_____

The most difficult part about the final waiting period was

_____

_____

_____

_____

_____

_____

_____

_____

_____

_____

_____

_____

_____

_____

I kept your spirit or presence with me by

_____

_____

_____

_____

_____

_____

_____

_____

_____

_____

_____

_____

The person(s) I chose to go with me to my first meeting with you and why:

_____

_____

_____

_____

_____

_____

_____

_____

_____

_____

_____

_____

_____

One special possession that I made sure to take with me was

_____
_____
_____
_____
_____
_____
_____
_____
_____
_____
_____
_____
_____

If I adopted internationally, the words that best describe the journey to your country are

_____
_____
_____
_____
_____
_____
_____
_____
_____
_____
_____
_____
_____
_____
_____
_____

If I adopted domestically, the words that best describe my drive or flight to our meeting place are

_____
_____
_____
_____
_____
_____
_____
_____
_____
_____
_____
_____

One final roadblock, setback, or challenge before your adoption became a reality was

_____
_____
_____
_____
_____
_____
_____
_____
_____
_____
_____
_____
_____
_____

I got through that by

_____
_____
_____
_____
_____
_____
_____
_____
_____
_____
_____
_____
_____
_____

God or spirit was helping to bring us together by

_____
_____
_____
_____
_____
_____
_____
_____
_____
_____
_____
_____
_____
_____
_____

Take a moment to reflect on the following qualities and the role they played during your Sacred Anticipation:

Patience:

Having patience was especially important when

_____

_____

Strength:

My strength was coming through in dealing with

_____

_____

Awe:

I was most filled with awe when

_____

_____

Cooperation:

I learned that cooperation was critical while preparing for adoption when

_____

_____

Faith:

I had to most rely on faith or trust about how your adoption would unfold when it came to

_____

_____

Use this page to add your own photos, drawings, inspirational messages, or other keepsakes that relate to Getting Ready for your adoption:

Sacred Celebration—Making It Happen

Think back to that unforgettable first visit or meeting with your child. Bring into focus the time, the place, the people, and everything else that touched your heart on that unforgettable day.

If I just learned that you would be my child when I arrived at my destination, I knew you were right for me by

_____

_____

_____

_____

_____

_____

What I most remember thinking or feeling when I first held or hugged you was

_____

_____

_____

_____

_____

_____

_____

The words I remember speaking, or wished I had said, were

_____
_____
_____
_____
_____
_____
_____
_____
_____
_____
_____
_____
_____
_____

What caught my eye about you right away was

_____
_____
_____
_____
_____
_____
_____
_____
_____
_____
_____
_____
_____
_____

Something else in the scene that filled me with awe or reverence was

_____
_____
_____
_____
_____
_____
_____
_____
_____
_____
_____
_____
_____
_____

This moment reminded me of

_____
_____
_____
_____
_____
_____
_____
_____
_____
_____
_____
_____
_____
_____

You first responded to me by

_____
_____
_____
_____
_____
_____
_____
_____
_____
_____
_____
_____
_____
_____
_____

My first clue about what life with you was going to be like was

_____
_____
_____
_____
_____
_____
_____
_____
_____
_____
_____
_____
_____
_____
_____
_____

If other loved ones were present, they responded to seeing you by

_____

_____

_____

_____

_____

_____

_____

_____

_____

_____

_____

I knew God or spirit was present in that room by

_____

_____

_____

_____

_____

_____

_____

_____

_____

_____

_____

_____

Now remember the moment you left the place where your adoption was completed. Try to recall everyone who was there and how you all said goodbye.

As we left, I most find myself noticing

_____

_____

_____

_____

_____

_____

_____

_____

_____

_____

_____

_____

If the birth mother was a part of the experience, what was expressed between us was

_____

_____

_____

_____

_____

_____

_____

_____

_____

_____

_____

_____

_____

If my child's caregivers or others were there, I tried to communicate my feelings toward them by

_____

_____

_____

_____

_____

_____

_____

_____

_____

_____

_____

_____

One special object I took with me, or wanted to take with me, to preserve the memory of this place for you was

_____

_____

_____

_____

_____

_____

_____

_____

_____

_____

_____

_____

If I could change one thing about that goodbye day, it would be to

_____
_____
_____
_____
_____
_____
_____
_____
_____
_____
_____
_____

Now focus in on the drive or trip going home together.

What felt different about going home compared to the trip going out was

_____
_____
_____
_____
_____
_____
_____
_____
_____
_____
_____
_____

The sights, sounds, or smells I recall are

_____
_____
_____
_____
_____
_____
_____
_____
_____
_____
_____
_____

What you handled well on the trip or ride home was

_____
_____
_____
_____
_____
_____
_____
_____
_____
_____
_____
_____

You may have struggled with

_____
_____
_____
_____
_____
_____
_____
_____
_____
_____
_____
_____
_____
_____
_____

God or spirit may have been helping by

_____
_____
_____
_____
_____
_____
_____
_____
_____
_____
_____
_____
_____
_____
_____

Close your eyes for a moment and re-visit Arrival Day: that moment when you got back home and your new family was born. Invite in all the details of what you saw, heard, and felt in coming home.

The people or signs waiting to greet us included

_____

_____

_____

_____

_____

_____

_____

_____

_____

_____

_____

What most touched me about this welcoming was

_____

_____

_____

_____

_____

_____

_____

_____

_____

_____

_____

_____

The most familiar or reassuring part about being back home was

_____
_____
_____
_____
_____
_____
_____
_____
_____
_____
_____
_____
_____
_____

One thing that already seemed different about home now was

_____
_____
_____
_____
_____
_____
_____
_____
_____
_____
_____
_____
_____
_____
_____
_____

What most captured your attention in your new surroundings was

_____
_____
_____
_____
_____
_____
_____
_____
_____
_____
_____
_____
_____
_____

Your sibling(s) or others responded to you by

_____
_____
_____
_____
_____
_____
_____
_____
_____
_____
_____
_____
_____
_____

The person(s) who got to hold or hug you first were

_____

_____

_____

_____

Seeing you with them made me feel

_____

_____

_____

_____

_____

_____

_____

_____

_____

_____

What I will never forget about those early visits, phone calls, or emails from friends and loved ones is

_____

_____

_____

_____

_____

_____

_____

_____

_____

_____

_____

In your first week at home with us, what gave me the most joy was

_____
_____
_____
_____
_____
_____
_____
_____
_____
_____
_____
_____

I had difficulty at times with

_____
_____
_____
_____
_____
_____
_____
_____
_____
_____
_____
_____

Perhaps your early period back home with your child included a blessing, christening, naming, or other ritual. If so, re-visit that experience now.

Your first ritual included these people and activities:

_____
_____
_____
_____
_____
_____
_____
_____
_____
_____
_____
_____
_____
_____

The one moment during that ritual that I will never forget was when

_____
_____
_____
_____
_____
_____
_____
_____
_____
_____
_____
_____
_____
_____

Take a moment to reflect on the following qualities and the role they played during your Sacred Celebration:

Gratitude:

In those first moments or days with you, I was filled with gratitude for

_____

_____

Amazement:

In bringing you into our life and our home, I found myself in total amazement over

_____

_____

Empathy:

In leaving the place where you were born, I felt the most empathy for

_____

_____

Joy:

I felt my heart rise with joy in first being with you because

_____

_____

Beauty:

Your beauty most shone through to me when

_____

_____

Use this page to add your own photos, drawings, inspirational messages, or other keepsakes that relate to Making Your Adoption Happen:

Sacred Beginnings—Starting a New Life

Think back to that first year with your adoptive child: all the hard work, all the fun, all the changes, all the frustration, all the surprises.

During that first year with you, what most filled me with awe and wonder was

_____

_____

_____

_____

_____

_____

_____

_____

What I found the most difficult or challenging was

_____

_____

_____

_____

_____

_____

_____

_____

_____

I met those challenges by

_____
_____
_____
_____
_____
_____
_____
_____
_____
_____
_____
_____
_____
_____
_____

One inspirational quotation or message guiding me was

_____
_____
_____
_____
_____
_____
_____
_____
_____
_____
_____
_____
_____
_____
_____

Something new in my understanding or appreciation of family was

_____

_____

_____

_____

_____

_____

_____

_____

_____

_____

_____

_____

_____

Something new in my approach to work, career, or life outside home was

_____

_____

_____

_____

_____

_____

_____

_____

_____

_____

_____

_____

_____

Something new in my old and new friendships was

_____
_____
_____
_____
_____
_____
_____
_____
_____
_____
_____
_____
_____

Something new in my connection to God or the sacred was

_____
_____
_____
_____
_____
_____
_____
_____
_____
_____
_____
_____
_____
_____

Now take a moment to consider all the many people who helped you during your adjustment period at home. Appreciate all the many ways they expressed their love, caring, and support.

The person most supporting me and what they did for me was

_____
_____
_____
_____
_____
_____
_____
_____
_____
_____
_____
_____

If I were to write a thank-you note to the closest person to me during this time, it would begin:

_____
_____
_____
_____
_____
_____
_____
_____
_____
_____
_____

Beyond family and close friends, the most appreciated gestures from our church, our adoption network, or our larger community were

_____
_____
_____
_____
_____
_____
_____
_____
_____
_____
_____
_____
_____
_____
_____

One event or experience that reminded me how God or spirit was supporting me in my new life with you was

_____
_____
_____
_____
_____
_____
_____
_____
_____
_____
_____
_____
_____
_____

Now reflect on how your child was responding to his or her adjustment in your life together.

What most seemed to make you happy in your new home was

_____
_____
_____
_____
_____
_____
_____
_____
_____
_____
_____

You had trouble with

_____
_____
_____
_____
_____
_____
_____
_____
_____
_____
_____
_____
_____

You related to other family members by

_____
_____
_____
_____
_____
_____
_____
_____
_____
_____
_____
_____
_____
_____
_____
_____

Your first new friends and what did you did together was

_____
_____
_____
_____
_____
_____
_____
_____
_____
_____
_____
_____
_____
_____
_____
_____

What you most seemed to enjoy learning or discovering was

_____

_____

_____

_____

_____

_____

_____

_____

_____

_____

_____

We celebrated your first birthday at home by

_____

_____

_____

_____

_____

_____

_____

_____

_____

_____

_____

_____

_____

_____

What I saw in you during your first year that most made me want to laugh was

_____
_____
_____
_____
_____
_____
_____
_____
_____
_____
_____
_____
_____
_____

What most made me want to cry was

_____
_____
_____
_____
_____
_____
_____
_____
_____
_____
_____
_____
_____
_____

My most memorable moment in your first year home was

_____
_____
_____
_____
_____
_____
_____
_____
_____
_____
_____
_____

One strange or scary moment was when

_____
_____
_____
_____
_____
_____
_____
_____
_____
_____
_____
_____
_____

We knew that God or spirit was present during that first year by

_____
_____
_____
_____
_____
_____
_____
_____
_____
_____
_____
_____
_____
_____
_____
_____
_____
_____
_____
_____
_____
_____
_____
_____
_____
_____
_____
_____
_____
_____
_____
_____
_____

Take a moment to reflect on the following qualities and the role they played during your Sacred Beginnings:

Love:

I especially felt love in the air when

_____

_____

_____

Understanding:

I learned just how important understanding would be when

_____

_____

_____

Perseverance:

I had to tap a new layer of perseverance in responding to

_____

_____

_____

Wonder:

I could just shake my head with wonder over how you

_____

_____

_____

Use this page to add your own photos, drawings, inspirational messages, or other keepsakes that relate to Starting a New Life together:

Sacred Commitment—Keeping Spirit Alive

You may choose to fill in this final section two, three, or several years into the experience of life with your child. To begin, reflect on the events of the day you just completed: the activities, the chores, the familiar, and the new. Consider how they fit the big picture.

As time has gone on, I see your spirits being especially lifted whenever you

_____

_____

_____

_____

_____

_____

_____

_____

You show love by

_____

_____

_____

_____

_____

_____

_____

_____

You seem to feel pain, sadness, or fear when

_____
_____
_____
_____
_____
_____
_____
_____
_____
_____
_____
_____
_____
_____
_____
_____

I try to help you deal with those feelings by

_____
_____
_____
_____
_____
_____
_____
_____
_____
_____
_____
_____
_____
_____
_____

I would describe the way you relate to other people and the world around you as

_____

_____

_____

_____

_____

_____

_____

_____

_____

_____

_____

_____

_____

_____

One time you did or said something that simply took my breath away was

_____

_____

_____

_____

_____

_____

_____

_____

_____

_____

_____

_____

_____

_____

I see your greatest strengths or gifts as

_____
_____
_____
_____
_____
_____
_____
_____
_____
_____
_____
_____
_____

As I think about your future, I see you impacting our family and the world around you through your

_____
_____
_____
_____
_____
_____
_____
_____
_____
_____
_____
_____
_____
_____

As I live with you day to day, I feel the most warmth and love when you

_____

_____

_____

_____

_____

_____

_____

_____

_____

_____

_____

_____

_____

I most see you as a reflection of God when

_____

_____

_____

_____

_____

_____

_____

_____

_____

_____

_____

_____

_____

One sacred gift I received from you in the past week is

_____
_____
_____
_____
_____
_____
_____
_____
_____
_____
_____
_____

My greatest wish about your future is

_____
_____
_____
_____
_____
_____
_____
_____
_____
_____
_____
_____
_____
_____
_____

My biggest fear or concern is

_____
_____
_____
_____
_____
_____
_____
_____
_____
_____
_____
_____
_____

The role that faith, or sacred trust, plays for me when I imagine your life ahead is

_____
_____
_____
_____
_____
_____
_____
_____
_____
_____
_____
_____
_____
_____
_____

When I consider your growth, something I hope I am doing well is

_____

_____

_____

_____

_____

_____

_____

_____

_____

_____

_____

_____

_____

I sometimes worry that I may be falling short in

_____

_____

_____

_____

_____

_____

_____

_____

_____

_____

_____

_____

_____

_____

_____

_____

An inspirational message that helps sustain me is

_____
_____
_____
_____
_____
_____
_____
_____
_____
_____
_____
_____
_____
_____
_____

A special game or song that gives me tingles when we share it is

_____
_____
_____
_____
_____
_____
_____
_____
_____
_____
_____
_____
_____
_____

I try to bring God or spirit into your life by

_____
_____
_____
_____
_____
_____
_____
_____
_____
_____
_____
_____
_____
_____
_____

You usually respond by

_____
_____
_____
_____
_____
_____
_____
_____
_____
_____
_____
_____
_____
_____

Next, reflect on the continued role of adoption in your shared life with your child.

When I approach the subject of adoption with you, what is sacred about that to me is

_____

_____

_____

_____

_____

_____

_____

_____

_____

_____

_____

_____

I try to honor your birth mother or cultural heritage by

_____

_____

_____

_____

_____

_____

_____

_____

_____

_____

_____

_____

We observe "Gotcha Day," or our way of acknowledging when you came into our life by

_____
_____
_____
_____
_____
_____
_____
_____
_____
_____
_____
_____
_____
_____

If I have contact with your birth mother, what means the most to me about that contact is

_____
_____
_____
_____
_____
_____
_____
_____
_____
_____
_____
_____
_____
_____
_____

If I do not have open contact with your birth mother, what I would want to express to her if I had the chance is

_____
_____
_____
_____
_____
_____
_____
_____
_____
_____
_____
_____
_____

My adoption experience with you has impacted my outlook toward adoption by

_____
_____
_____
_____
_____
_____
_____
_____
_____
_____
_____
_____
_____

What I would *most* want to say to someone considering adoption is

_____
_____
_____
_____
_____
_____
_____
_____
_____
_____
_____
_____
_____

Think about one favorite ritual or activity that you regularly engage in with your child. It could be something as simple as a bath, sharing an ice cream, or a bedtime prayer. Consider the details of what you both do and say during that treasured experience.

The most touching part of this experience to me is

_____
_____
_____
_____
_____
_____
_____
_____
_____
_____
_____
_____

What it seems to mean to you is

_____

_____

_____

_____

_____

_____

_____

_____

_____

_____

_____

_____

_____

_____

One special way we say goodnight together is

_____

_____

_____

_____

_____

_____

_____

_____

_____

_____

_____

_____

_____

We often say hello when we get back together after time apart by

_____
_____
_____
_____
_____
_____
_____
_____
_____
_____
_____
_____
_____
_____
_____

One new ritual we might add to our life soon is

_____
_____
_____
_____
_____
_____
_____
_____
_____
_____
_____
_____
_____
_____

Parenting any child is, of course, a sacred endeavor. Consider what this means to you today as it relates to your experience as an adoptive parent.

I would describe the sacred voice or guidance that supports me as

_____
_____
_____
_____
_____
_____
_____
_____
_____
_____
_____
_____

One message from that voice that really inspires me is

_____
_____
_____
_____
_____
_____
_____
_____
_____
_____
_____
_____

My whole adoption experience has been a miracle to me because

_____
_____
_____
_____
_____
_____
_____
_____
_____
_____
_____
_____
_____
_____
_____
_____

If I were to write a letter from the heart to you, my child, about what it means to have you in my life, it would begin:

_____
_____
_____
_____
_____
_____
_____
_____
_____
_____
_____
_____
_____
_____
_____
_____
_____

Take a moment to reflect on the following qualities and the role they play in your Sacred Commitment:

Playfulness:

I feel my own playfulness joining with you when we

_____

_____

_____

Respect:

I feel the deepest respect for you when

_____

_____

_____

Healing:

The healing that I have experienced through our adoption is about

_____

_____

_____

Compassion:

I now have much more compassion for

_____

_____

_____

Inspiration:

Having you in my life is an inspiration because

_____
_____
_____
_____
_____
_____

Devotion:

As you get older, my devotion to keeping God or spirit alive in our lives means that

_____
_____
_____
_____
_____
_____

Fill in the blank at the end of this statement with your first thought:

I know the sacred is present in our life together by

_____
_____
_____
_____
_____
_____

Use this page to add your own photos, drawings, inspirational messages, or other keepsakes that relate to Keeping Spirit Alive:

About the Author

Kevin Quirk is dedicated to helping people preserve their life stories, especially their most meaningful experiences. He teaches writing classes at the University of Virginia School of Continuing Education and Professional Studies, and the Osher Lifelong Learning Institute at the University of Virginia. He also assists individual clients write and publish books as a ghostwriter, interviewer, editor, advisor, and publishing coach through Memoirs for Life.

A former journalist, Kevin is the author of *Not Now, Honey, I'm Watching the Game* (Simon & Schuster/Fireside), which was featured by ABC's 20/20, National Public Radio, *Redbook, Men's Health, Sports Illustrated,* ESPN, Good Day New York, *The Washington Post, The Dallas Morning News, The Boston Globe,* and dozens of other radio and TV programs throughout the U.S. and Canada. As an adoptive parent, he also is the author of *Hello, Aibek! A Journey of International Adoption.* He is the ghostwriter or editor for several other books.

A native of Shrewsbury, Massachusetts, Kevin has a B.S. in Journalism from Boston University, an M.A. in Writing from the University of New Hampshire, and an M.A. in Spiritual Psychology from Holy Names College. He currently lives with his wife Krista and son Aibek in Charlottesville, Virginia. He can be reached via email at: kevin@memoirsforlife.com.

978-0-595-48530-7
0-595-48530-8

LaVergne, TN USA
18 December 2009
167585LV00001B/109/P